NIJINSKY ON STAGE

NIJINSKY
ON STAGE

Action drawings by Valentine Gross
of Nijinsky and the Diaghilev Ballet
made in Paris between 1909 and 1913,
being a donation to the Museum of Theatre Arts, London
by Jean Hugo

With a Chronology by Jean Hugo,
and an Introduction and Notes
by Richard Buckle

STUDIO VISTA

Produced by November Books Limited, 23–29 Emerald Street, London WC1N 3QL.

Published by Studio Vista Publishers, Blue Star House, Highgate Hill, London N19.

Text set by Perfect Typesetters Limited, 5–7 City Garden Row, London N1 8DP.

Printed by Flarepath Printers Limited, Watling Street, St Albans, Hertfordshire.

Bound by Dorstel Press Limited, West Road, Templefields, Harlow, Essex.

© November Books Limited 1971.

First published 1971.

House Editor: Frances Kennett.

ISBN 0 289 70202 x

Contents

Acknowledgements

Mme Lydia Sokolova, always the most generous and helpful of friends, gave me invaluable assistance in identifying certain poses in *Les Sylphides, Daphnis et Chloë* and *Le Sacre du printemps*. Mme Karsavina was kind enough to give me her thoughts about the drawings of *L'Oiseau de feu*. I thank them most sincerely. R.B.

Chronology
Of The Life Of
Valentine Gross

1887   16 March: born at Capécure, suburb of Boulogne-sur-mer, the daughter of Auguste Gross and Zélie Demelin, and christened Valentine Marie Augustine.

c. 1892–1907   Educated first by her aunt, Mlle Augusta Gross, schoolmistress at Boulogne, then at a school for English girls at Boulogne, where she learns no word of English. Wins prizes for drawing.

1907   Enters Ecole des Beaux-Arts, Paris. Lives first at a *pension de famille*, then in rooms in the rue des Beaux-Arts.

1909   Still at the Ecole des Beaux-Arts, where she studies at the Atelier Humbert. Wins *seconde médaille d'esquisse peinte*. Meets Aman-Jean, who paints her portrait. Exhibits at the Salon des Artistes Français and is awarded a '*mention*'. Moves to 29 quai de Bourbon, Ile St Louis. Meets Jérome and Jean Tharaud and Charles de Pesloüan. First Russian Season (of opera and ballet) at the Châtelet.

1910   Wins prix Hautmont at the Ecole des Beaux-Arts. Russian Season at the Opéra.

1911   Exhibits at the Salon des Artistes français. Russian Season at the Châtelet and a few performances around Christmas at the Opéra.

1912   Russian Season at the Châtelet.

1913   Meets Jacques de Brunhoff (*Comoedia Illustré*) and Lucien Vogel (*Gazette du Bon Ton*). Meets Misia and Cypa Godebski, Roger de la Fresnaye, Léon-Paul Fargue, Gaston Gallimard (*Nouvelle Revue Française*), Erik Satie. Russian Season at the Champs-Elysées. Exhibits 100 pastels in foyer of theatre. Pastels of *Jeux* published in *Comoedia Illustré*. Marriage and dismissal of Nijinsky.

1914   Meets Jean Cocteau. Russian Season (without Nijinsky) at the Opéra. Drawings of Karsavina in *Coq d'or* published in *Comoedia Illustré* and *Gazette du Bon Ton*. Contributes pastels to an exhibition of portraits of Nijinsky at the Fine Arts, Bond Street, London. Publication by Brunhoff of her *Mouvements de la danse de l'Antiquité à nos jours* stopped by the war. One chapter published in *Revue archéologique*. Her portrait by Aman-Jean shown at the Salon.

1915   Meets Georges Auric. Monotypes, lino-cuts. Betrothed to Charles Stern.

1916   Meets Picasso.

1917   Meets Jean Hugo, great-grandson of Victor Hugo. Moves to 28 rue Montpensier, Palais Royal.

1919   Meets Raymond Radiguet.
        7 August: marries Jean Hugo; Satie and Cocteau being her witnesses.

1920   Paints portrait of Pavlova.

1921   Helps Jean Hugo execute the costumes for *Les Mariés de la Tour Eiffel*, Ballet Suédois.

1922   Holiday at Lavandou with Cocteau, Radiguet and her husband. Moves to 11 rue Chateaubriand, Champs-Elysées. Publishes an article on 'La Danse théâtrale pendant la Révolution française' in *La Revue Musicale*.

1923   Visits the sick Nijinsky at Passy and goes with him and Romola Nijinsky to the ballet. Holiday at Piquey with Cocteau, Radiguet, Auric.
        12 December: death of Radiguet.

1924   Helps Jean Hugo execute the costumes for *Roméo et Juliette* by Cocteau for the *Soirées de Paris* of Comte Etienne de Beaumont at Théâtre de la Cigale.

1925   Moves to Avenue de Lamballe, Passy.

1926   First steps towards surrealism.
        15 June: *Orphée* by Cocteau at Théâtre des Arts-Pitoeff marks the end of her friendship with Cocteau.

1927   Helps Carl Dreyer in the films *La Passion de Jeanne d'Arc* (costumes by Jean Hugo) and *Les Vampires*.

1928   Moves to rue Vignon, near the Madeleine.

1929   Parts from Jean Hugo.

1930   Makes friends with Eluard and Breton.

1931   Holiday with Eluard and Breton in Brittany and

the Provençal Alps. Moves to rue Montpensier, Palais Royal. Paints portraits of the surrealist poets Eluard, Breton, Tzara, Crevel, Char (Matarasso Collection).

1933 Exhibits at the Salon des Surindépendants, with the Surrealist group. Illustrates *Contes bizarres* by Achim von Arnim. Moves to rue Fontaine, Montmartre.

1936 Moves to 2 rue de Sontay, windows opening on Place Victor Hugo.

1937 Illustrates *Appliquée* by Eluard (7 etchings) and *Placard pour un chemin des écoliers* by Char.

1938 Illustrates *Les Animaux et leurs hommes* by Eluard (etchings) and *Les poètes de sept ans* by Rimbaud (7 etchings).

1939 Illustrates *Médiouses* by Eluard (35 lithographs) and *Ondine* by La Motte-Fouqué.

1940 Illustrates *Blason des fleurs et des fruits* by Eluard (1 woodcut).

1941 November: décor and costumes for *La Fille du Jardinier* by Charles Exbrayat, Théâtre des Mathurins.

1946 Décor and costumes for *Primavera* by Claude Spaak.

1947 14 June: décor and costumes for *Pelléas et Mélisande* at the Opéra comique, severely criticised. Illustrates *Corps mémorable* by Eluard and *Deux Coeurs simples* by Jacques de Lacretelle.

1948 25 October: finishes portrait of Picasso begun in October 1934.

1950 8 April: death of Nijinsky.

1951 Illustrates *Le Phénix* by Eluard (18 drawings).

1952 Décor for *Pelléas*, second version.
18 November: death of Eluard.

1955 Makes friends with Brancusi.

1956 16 March: death of Brancusi.

1963 11 October: death of Cocteau.

1966 28 September: death of Breton.
Contributes *collages* to a Diaghilev exhibition in the foyer of the Théâtre des Champs Elysées.

1968 Dies on her birthday, 16 March, rue de Sontay.

Introduction

In May 1909, Diaghilev brought Russian ballet to Paris for the first time and it struck nearly all who saw it as an incredible new form of art. Fokine's revolutionary ideas of choreography, the designs of Alexandre Benois, Nicolas Roerich and Leon Bakst, Borodin's barbaric music for *Prince Igor*, the poetry of *Les Sylphides*, the drama of *Cléopâtre*, the dancing of Karsavina and Nijinsky – all these were overwhelming.

Among those present at the famous *répétition générale* on 18 May was the young art student, Valentine Gross. She was just a year older than Nijinsky, who had graduated from the Imperial Theatre School in Petersburg two years before. She was spellbound by the Russians, and by Nijinsky in particular, and from that day she never missed a performance during the annual Russian seasons in Paris up to the outbreak of war. Moreover, she began to draw the dancers in action. It could be said that she had found her vocation, for although she never saw Nijinsky dance after 1913 – he became mentally ill in 1918 – and although she was to have other interests than ballet and to make pictures of other subjects than dancers, she continued throughout her life to plan a history of the dance from earliest times, and to collect materials for a book on Nijinsky.

The motive, of course, behind the tireless jottings of Valentine Gross, was to record a series of uplifting theatrical experiences, to chronicle a golden age of dancing, in the way that Chalon, Brandard and other artists and lithographers had recorded the ballerinas of the Romantic era in London three-quarters of a century before. Her notes made in the theatre and in the dark could be called unconscious, because she did not know what or how she was drawing. Together with the scribbled name of a dancer or the colour of a costume they were an *aide-mémoire* which might turn out to be legible and helpful, or, as happened in a number of cases, might not. She would not consider these notes as drawings and would probably shrink from showing them to anyone else. But she would make other more detailed drawings from them, see the ballet again, correct her studies, trace and retrace them, and finally compose a 'finished' watercolour – or, far more often, a pastel. These pastels were exhibited and sold; and some of them were reproduced in the souvenir programmes of the Russian Ballet published by *Comoedia Illustré* or in magazines.

Popular in their day – and Nijinsky at least *said* he liked them, while Diaghilev's colleague, the critic Svetlov, bought them – the pastels have tended to seem during the past half century of experiment in art, increasingly absurd. Valentine Gross, as Jean Hugo has said to me, was an academic artist; she was aware of this and struggled all her life not to be one. But fashions change and there are signs that her finished drawings, watercolours and pastels are beginning to find admirers again. This may be because of their *art nouveau* quality, because of their period flavour, or simply because they often represent the legendary Nijinsky. Who could have guessed ten years ago that these works of Valentine Gross might fetch in a sale – as happened at Sotheby's in 1967, 1968 and 1969 – several hundred pounds each?[1] As her

[1] Or, for that matter, that one of the water-colours of Nijinsky by Georges Barbier, made for the album he published in 1913 with a preface by Francis de Miomandre, and in whose fantastic distortions *à la* Beardsley there were not even the evidences of first-hand observation which works of Valentine Gross never lacked, should sell for £900 !

works grow more finished and idealised, so they become sentimental and lacking in vitality: and even when her eye for form and movement remains faithful, her colouring tends towards a generalised bluey-greeny-pinkiness, so that the décors of Bakst, Benois and Roerich might all be the work of one artist. In fact, whatever ballet she is depicting, she never fails to produce an identifiable Valentine Gross.

Such is not the case with the 'unconscious' drawings made in the theatre: in these the artist is anonymous. Some have artistic merits, others have not. Many give a vivid impression of the quality of a movement or of an emotion portrayed. As the artist's eyes follow the figure of Nijinsky on stage, she does not know whether her hand is drawing head, neck, arm or costume. Very often it is drawing none of these, but inventing – with the speed born of necessity – a symbol for movement. Several times, in the scribbles of Les Sylphides, Valentine Gross is extraordinarily lucky in conveying the twist of a head and the sweep of an arm – the very subtleties on which the poetry of Fokine depends. In her drawings of Nijinsky's experimental L'Après-midi d'un faune, the choreography of which was unlike anything that had been seen before, she grasped instinctively (almost as if they had talked it over) his attempt to dehumanise the body and treat it as the element of an angular composition. In these two ballets, as in all her theatre drawings, Valentine Gross is recording movements or poses; in her more evolved studies of Nijinsky in Schéhérazade she is also portraying abandon; while in the sketches of Nijinsky in Petrushka, which are neither as elementary as the Sylphides drawings nor as considered as the Schéhérazade ones, so that we cannot tell whether they were done during a performance or after one,[2] she depicts passion. The puppet's dejection, his brief pang of joy at the appearance of the Ballerina, and his final cri du coeur before death are feelingly observed. In these drawings a little of Nijinsky in his famous role lives on for ever.

[2] They were possibly done, it occurs to me, at a rehearsal.

As will be evident from the preceding remarks, drawings in various stages of evolution are included in this book – all except the final, decorative pastels. Most are of the very first shorthand stage – and these must have, I feel, for a student an awe-inspiring aspect, since they were made at the Châtelet, at the Opéra or at the Théâtre des Champs-Elysées from life, in the very presence of Nijinsky, Karsavina and Nijinska, while they danced. There are only a few in the second, third and semi-final stages.

Apart from finished works in museums or collections, there may exist other notebooks or loose drawings by Valentine Gross similar to those reproduced here; or these, if they once existed, may have been destroyed. All those illustrated have – with one exception – been given by M. Jean Hugo to the Museum of Theatre Arts in London. The exception, included for the sake of illustrating Nijinsky as Harlequin in *Carnaval*, was bought for the Museum at a Sotheby sale.

Nijinsky is here shown in most of his important roles. It is curious, incidentally, that there should exist so many sketches (not all of which are illustrated) of Nijinsky as Daphnis in Fokine's *Daphnis et Chloë*, a role he only danced twice. We have nothing of him, however, in Fokine's *Pavillon d'Armide* or *Narcisse* or *Le Dieu bleu*; nothing in the Petipa *pas de deux*, *L'Oiseau bleu* (to which Diaghilev gave a variety of names), and nothing in his own *Jeux* – seven pastels of which are well-known. In compensation, we can produce records of Nijinsky's and Stravinsky's masterpiece, *Le Sacre du printemps*, which only had seven performances (four in Paris, three in London), and in which the choreographer did not himself appear. In this astonishing work, so far ahead of its time, Nijinsky the choreographer may be said to have sired the whole movement of Modern Dance. The drawings of it by Valentine Gross, a few of which are now shown to the world for the first time, have therefore a value which it is hard to over-estimate. Dancers, choreographers and historians must for ever be grateful to her for the pains she took.

THE DRAWINGS

Les Sylphides

Les Sylphides

Music: Chopin, orchestrated Liadov, Glazunov, Taneev, Sokolov and Stravinsky. Choreography: Fokine. Décor: Benois.

The lighting.

The decor of a romantic grove with a ruined Gothic church is indicated so cursorily as to be unrecognisable: more interesting, however – and it is confirmed on other sketches not included here – are the artist's notes on the colours of the lighting. To us, who are accustomed nowadays to an overall, bluish moonlight effect in this famous and perennially popular ballet, it comes as a surprise to study the record of Valentine Gross. On the backcloth of night sky she writes '*bleu mauve*'; there is a band of '*vert*' upstage, then, apparently, a bar of shadow across the centre. The foreground is clearly divided: to the left '*jaune*'; to the right '*vert*'. If Diaghilev was responsible for the lighting, or if he worked on it with Benois, it is startlingly clear that he or they brought to the Petersburg designer's pastiche Romantic setting a glow of Impressionism, which we should associate far more with advanced Moscow painters and stage-designers, such as Golovine and Korovine.

17

Les Sylphides

Nocturne. Karsavina and Nijinsky.

Les Sylphides was first given in Paris during the second mixed programme of ballet and opera in the first famous season at the Théâtre du Châtelet on 2 June 1909. It marked the début in Paris of Anna Pavlova, who had missed the previous ten days of the season. Her solo was the Mazurka (op. 33, no. 2) and she danced the Valse *pas de deux* (op. 64, no. 2) with Nijinsky. Karsavina danced the first solo, the Valse (op. 70, no. 1), which followed the opening Nocturne (op. 32, no. 2), Baldina the Prelude (op. 28, no. 7), and Nijinsky, of course, the only male solo, a Mazurka (op. 67, no. 3). After the *pas de deux* Valse, all joined in the final Valse brillante (op. 18), which had been orchestrated by Diaghilev's new friend, Stravinsky.

Among the selection from the artist's many sketches for *Les Sylphides* included here, none shows Pavlova, who did not appear with Diaghilev in Paris after 1909. It is therefore safe to assume that the drawings (comprising at least two notebooks) were made at the Opéra in 1910 or at the Châtelet in 1911. The ballet was not given during the short Paris season at the Châtelet in 1912, and in 1913, Bronislava Nijinska was pregnant. She occurs in these drawings, replacing Pavlova in the solo Mazurka. Although Karsavina always retained her solo Valse, she would, as ballerina of the company, dance the *pas de deux* Valse with Nijinsky after the departure of Pavlova. There is, however, one drawing of Bronislava Nijinska in the *pas de deux*.

Nijinsky lifts Karsavina in the opening Nocturne. To the right, another vague impression of the stage, which suggests that the artist was seated high up in the house to the right of centre.

Les Sylphides

Nocturne. Karsavina and Nijinsky.

As Nijinsky supports Karsavina by her right hand, (she is in an *arabesque* facing left), the artist has caught an impression of his ballooning white silk sleeves.

Les Sylphides
Nocturne. Karsavina and Nijinsky.
Three sketches. They circle the stage, jumping.

Les Sylphides

Nocturne. Bronislava Nijinska.

This is the moment when all the Sylphs execute undulating
port de bras with their backs to the audience.

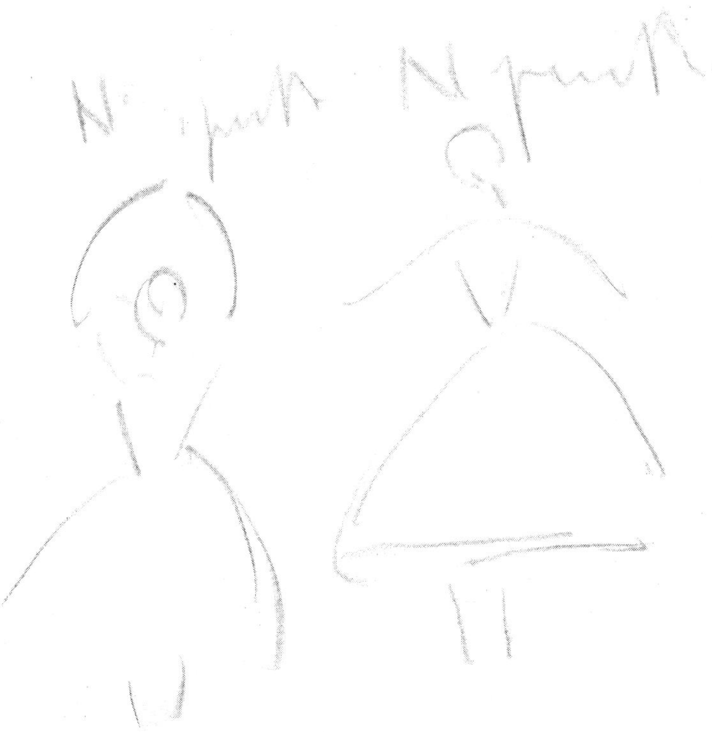

Right

Les Sylphides

Nocturne. Bronislava Nijinska, Karsavina and Nijinsky.

The male dancer supports the two principal ballerinas as they lean outward from him in a *demi-attitude*. Inscribed 'Nijinska fleurs bleus' and 'Nijinska et (?) Karsavina': Karsavina would be the only woman whose wreath was of pink flowers.

Left

Les Sylphides

Nocturne. Bronislava Nijinska, Karsavina, Nijinsky; and Nijinsky alone.

In the drawing to the left, the male dancer supports the two ballerinas at the moment before they break away and run to either side of the stage. The expressive hieroglyph on the right shows Nijinsky alone in the centre. He extends his arms in one yearning gesture before running off to leave the stage clear for Karsavina's Valse.

Les Sylphides

Valse. Karsavina and *corps de ballet*.

In the left-hand drawing, the dancer is shown alone, in a momentary pause in her flight across the stage. On the right, in an extraordinarily revealing shorthand statement, she is drawn poised against two members of the *corps* – one standing, one kneeling – in the background. (The impression that Karsavina is linked to them is illusory – the result of the artist's scribbling in the dark.) Why is this rapid sketch of Karsavina on the right so 'revealing'? It shows by luck and by skill the relation of the ballerina's back-curved body to the firm vertical stem of her left leg, the noble and poetic backward tilt of her head and the typically Fokinish drifting motion – it is not a pose – of her arms: all this without the proper delineation of a single limb. Here occidental drawing (in the dark, without looking down) approaches the pictograms of Chinese calligraphy, which marry words with visual art.

Right

Les Sylphides

Mazurka. B. Nijinska.

At the beginning of this rapid windswept dance, the soloist makes three false entries in diagonal, crossing the stage and leaving it before eventually resigning herself to come on through an arch formed by the arms of the *corps*, back centre, and to remain on stage and dance. This may have been sketched during one of her preliminary flits.

Left

Les Sylphides

Valse. Karsavina.

One of the 'unclassical' innovations of Fokine's choreography – although *Les Sylphides* contained far more classical steps than most of his dance-dramas – was to allow the ballerina to turn her back to the audience. This would have been unthinkable in a Petipa ballet.

Here Karsavina raises her arms *en couronne* over her head as she performs an *arabesque* in diagonal away from the audience and her tulle skirts rise frothily above her waist.

Right

Les Sylphides

Mazurka. B. Nijinska.

If the two right arms (on the left) were eliminated from the left-hand drawing with its four arms, and the figure were reversed, it could be compared to the proud pose of Serov's drawing of Pavlova in *Les Sylphides* which was used in 1909 as the first poster of Diaghilev's Russian seasons in Paris.

In the right-hand drawing, the raised right shoulder and expressive arm combined with the uptilted head, appears to be that of a creature rapt and spellbound by the night (a mood more particularly associated with the dancer of the Prelude which follows, and of which we have no drawing). Elementary as it is, the pose conveys the very essence of Fokine's '*rêverie chorégraphique*'.

Left

Les Sylphides

Mazurka. B. Nijinska.

The artist has tried to record a beaten step of the feet and the flickering undulation of the arms. To the right, a sketch of Nijinska's coiffure and wreath in profile. From the note on another sketch (see page 24) we know she wore blue flowers.

Right

Les Sylphides

Valse *pas de deux.* Karsavina and Nijinsky.

As she trips round the stage he follows her, executing back *cabrioles.*

Left

Les Sylphides

Valse *pas de deux*. Karsavina and Nijinsky.

The left-hand drawing is of the two dancers' entrance,
upstage left. Nijinsky, rather than lifting the ballerina
on to the stage, appears to be catching her as she alights
from the trees.

Right

Les Sylphides

Valse *pas de deux*. Karsavina and Nijinsky.

As the ballerina trips backwards, executing *pas de bourrée* in a diagonal and undulating her arms, the male dancer appears to be drawing her back by her wings, at the same time beating his legs gently behind him. The artist has attempted to indicate these movements.

Left

Les Sylphides

Valse *pas de deux*. Karsavina and Nijinsky.

Just before the dance ends, Nijinsky combines his *cabrioles* with single turns in the air, without letting go of Karsavina's hand as she runs after him on point.

Les Sylphides

Valse *pas de deux*. Nijinska and Nijinsky.

On the night this was drawn, Bronislava Nijinska and not Karsavina was dancing the *pas de deux*. Just before the exit; her back is turned (as the artist's inscription indicates).

Schéhérazade

Schéhérazade

Music : Rimsky-Korsakov. Choreography : Fokine. Decor : Bakst.

The Golden Slave and the Sultana Zobeïda. Nijinsky and Karsavina.

After the King and his suspicious brother have gone out hunting, the Chief Eunuch is bribed to unlock the doors into the slaves' quarters and the women of the harem are united in an orgy with their negro lovers.

The role of Zobeïda was created by Ida Rubinstein on the first night of the Russian Season at the Paris Opera, in 1910, when the sadistic dance-drama in its overpowering setting by Bakst caused a sensation. In 1911, when Diaghilev had his own company – as opposed to a company of the Tsar's dancers working for him during their vacation – Karsavina took over the role. This drawing would therefore have been made in 1911, 1912 or 1913.

More than one observer has commented that when Nijinsky was 'making love' to Karsavina, although his flickering hands appeared to be on the point of enfolding her in ecstatic embraces, he never actually touched her body. This no doubt considerably enhanced the fantastic nature of their love-making, but the real reason may have been to prevent his dark make-up discolouring her white arms and flimsy jewelled costume.

Schéhérazade

The Golden Slave. Nijinsky.

The dancer wore gold *lamé* trousers, bunched up at the waist and attached by ropes of pearls in his jewelled *brassière*. In the early days of the ballet, the Negroes wore brown leotards to cover their arms and torso, painting only their hands and faces. Later the bodies were made-up – a more laborious process, but with more effective result – and Nijinsky painted himself a silver-prune colour.

Did Nijinsky dance on point? No historian has commented, I believe, until the appearance of this work and my biography, on how many photographs and drawings of Nijinsky show him on the very tips of his toes, like a female dancer. I asked Nijinsky's sister, Mme Bronislava Nijinska, about this and she said: "He only gave the appearance of being on point, only rose on to point momentarily."

There is no problem for a male dancer with strong feet to rise and move on his toes, but it is usually considered aesthetically displeasing. In 1913 Nijinsky began rehearsing his own ballet *Jeux* in blocked shoes, but abandoned the idea. Since then other male dancers have danced on point to create a special effect, notably Anton Dolin as the Dandy in Nijinska's *Les Fâcheux* in 1924, and Alexander Grant as Bottom transformed into an ass in Ashton's *The Dream* in 1964.

In certain photographs of Nijinsky as the Golden Slave, however, it can be seen that his gold shoes, without being blocked or having flat ends like women's, were elongated and padded at the tip. So many of his roles were not quite human – the simian Slave of *Schéhérazade*, the feline Harlequin of *Carnaval*, the sexless Rose in *Le Spectre de la rose*, the Puppet with a soul in *Petrushka*: in all of these he was portrayed on point by Valentine Gross and other artists.

Having made a poor sketch of the right hand, the artist draws it again in two different positions just below.

In the 1930s when Fokine was teaching the role of the Slave to André Eglevsky, the latter, whose English was

then less perfect than it later became, described to me the choreographer's instructions. "Fokine always say 'The Negro, he is glad of himself'." This drawing by Valentine Gross well expresses Nijinsky's rendering of that euphoric state.

42

Schéhérazade

The Golden Slave. Nijinsky.

In this and the two subsequent drawings, Nijinsky has been sketched joining in the general orgy.

Schéhérazade

The Golden Slave. Nijinsky.

The dancer has the same ecstatically backwards and side-
ways tilted head as in the last sketch but one.

Schéhérazade

The Golden Slave. Nijinsky.

Surely an image of dancing at its most Dionysian and
dithyrambic. In his own choreography, Nijinsky was to
react against such uninhibited abandon.

47

L'Oiseau de feu

L'Oiseau de feu (*Firebird*)

Music: Stravinsky. Choreography: Fokine. Decor: Golovine. Costumes: Golovine and Bakst.

The Firebird. Karsavina.

Three movements or poses are sketched here. In the first, the bird of fire is seen in the opening solo dance of Stravinsky's first ballet (also his first music to be heard in the west), darting flame-like through the darkness surrounding the castle of the evil sorcerer. In the second and third, standing and kneeling, she clasps herself tremulously at the approach of Prince Ivan (Fokine), who has climbed the wall and penetrated into the fearful place.

L'Oiseau de feu

The Firebird. Karsavina.

This page of drawings in Indian ink carries the first sketch on the previous page a stage further; has two variations on the second sketch; omits the kneeling third and introduces a fourth pose: back turned, with undulating arms.

L'Oiseau de feu

The Firebird. Karsavina.

A detailed drawing in pencil and watercolour of the sketches on the two previous pages. It shows the bird of fire soaring through the garden alone at the beginning of the ballet. In the original, the colours of her diaphanous green costume with red and orange ostrich and cock's feathers are indicated.

When I showed several coloured sketches by Valentine Gross to Mme Karsavina, she picked this one as the most truthful impression.

Carnaval

Carnaval

Music: Schumann, orchestrated by Rimsky-Korsakov, Liadov, Glazunov and Tcherepnine. Choreography: Fokine. Décor: Bakst.

Pierrot and Harlequin. Adolf Bolm and Nijinsky.

Probably the moment shortly before the final curtain, when Harlequin, who has made a fool of Pierrot, persuades him to be friends.

This is, of course, not a note made in the theatre, but something worked up afterwards, half-way to becoming a decorative composition. Although the artist has elongated Nijinsky in such a way as to make him appear tall (when he was only 5ft 4in), she has captured the raised knee position typical of the role and her drawing of the head reminds us of Nijinsky's uncanny rapid head-wagging, which everyone remarked upon.

Of Bolm's Pierrot, Cyril Beaumont wrote he 'was a tragic figure thrust outside the world of beauty and gaiety which he longed to enter'.

Nijinsky did not dance Harlequin when Diaghilev first presented Carnaval in 1910; he took over the role in 1911, performing it on the opening night at the Châtelet on 4 June. On 20 June, the Diaghilev Ballet appeared for the first time in England, and that night at Covent Garden Nijinsky danced in Le Pavillon d'Armide and Carnaval. The Schumann ballet was not given in Paris in 1912, but Valentine Gross would have had a last chance to see Nijinsky as Harlequin at the Champs-Elysées in 1913.

This is the only drawing included in the book not forming part of Jean Hugo's donation to the Museum of Theatre Arts. It was bought for the Museum at a Sotheby sale on 8 July 1969.

59

Le Spectre de la rose

Le Spectre de la rose

Libretto: Vaudoyer. Music: Weber, arranged Berlioz. Choreography: Fokine. Décor: Bakst.

The Rose and the Girl. Nijinsky and Karsavina.

The Girl, dressed in a white crinoline of 1840s fashion, returns from her first ball, and enters, sniffing the rose her partner gave her. She falls into a dreaming sleep in her armchair, letting the rose drop to the floor. The embodied spirit or fragrance of the rose bounds in at the window, to join her in the waltz of her dream.

To the right, a slight sketch of Karsavina asleep in the chair. To the left, Nijinsky in his pinkish-purple tights sewn with rose petals, executes *temps de poisson* to one of the several waltz tunes which make up the twelve-minute score.

Right
Le Spectre de la rose
The Rose and the Girl. Nijinsky and Karsavina.
The male dancer swings the ballerina over his head.

Left

Le Spectre de la rose

The Rose and the Girl. Nijinsky and Karsavina.

Having awoken the Girl with a kiss – awoken her not to the reality of waking life but to a state of entranced somnambulism, for she will dance with closed eyes – Nijinsky kneels to watch Karsavina rise on her toes as if yawning and prepare to relive the vertigo of the waltz.

Above

Le Spectre de la rose

The Rose and the Girl. Nijinsky and Karsavina.

Having returned the Girl to her armchair, the Rose, at a climax of the music, flings himself recumbent at her feet to gaze back at her over his shoulder with the ephemeral yearning of a soulless sylph.

Below

Le Spectre de la rose

The Rose and the Girl. Nijinsky and Karsavina.

Nijinsky implants a fairy kiss on the forehead of Karsavina before turning to take the little run which ends in the famous flight out of the window.

A poor scribble by Valentine Gross of the exit jump survives, but I have not included it. The marvel of this much-publicised *grand jeté*, following as it did on the longest non-stop dance in the ballet repertory, was not the measurable height Nijinsky soared from the ground but the artistry by which he contrived to give the impression that, having once taken off with an infinite continuity of grace, he was never going to come down, but would continue up and up, traversing 'some melodious plot of beechen green and shadows numberless' to arrive in the domain of Keats's nightingale.

Le Spectre de la rose

Curtain call. Karsavina and Nijinsky.

Nijinsky holds Karsavina's left hand, and extends his own left, as she curtseys deeply and he inclines his head with a modest acknowledgement. Taking the weight on his right leg, he trails his left in a somewhat effeminate way, which is more in keeping with his role in *Le Spectre* than that in *L'Après-midi d'un faune* (see page 105). Extra little sketches of the two dancers' heads are included above.

Petrushka

Petrushka

Music: Stravinsky. Choreography: Fokine. Décor: Benois.

Karsavina making up, 1.

Tamara Karsavina is sketched in her dressing-room at the Châtelet, making up for the role of the Ballerina or Doll. She is wearing a dressing-jacket trimmed with pom-poms which has nothing to do with Benois's costume for her role. Before applying her make-up, she has tied a scarf round her hair and is tucking in an escaped strand with what might be a knitting-needle.

petrouchka

Petrushka

Karsavina making up, 2.

She has removed the scarf, arranged her hair, and surveys the finished result of her make-up. The red spot is in place on the cheek – evidently not too exactly round (to be in keeping with Benois's scenery which was freely painted); and the black eyelashes have been applied in childish strokes, which will give a mindless doll-like look to her beautiful, dark eyes. While the dancer studies her face in the mirror the artist catches her noble profile, which the grotesque make-up cannot hide.

Petrushka

Karsavina making up, 3.

She has put on her pink velvet cap with its upturned rim
of white rabbit fur and is touching up the red blob on
her right cheekbone. Above, the artist has drawn
Karsavina's mouth full-face.

Petrushka

Scene I. The Fair.

Petrushka on his stand. Nijinsky.

The Magician has parted the curtains of his booth, revealing to the crowd its three compartments in which his puppets, the Moor, the Ballerina and Petrushka are on display, supported under the arms by padded metal stands. Nijinsky as Petrushka, who is about to be galvanised into life (the last of the three) by a touch of the Magician's flute, to reveal that he has developed a rudimentary soul and suffers for love of the Ballerina, sags like a sawdust thing. He wears a garish red and white smock, checked magenta and yellow trousers and boots like black wooden stumps.

Petrushka was first given at the Châtelet on 13 June 1911. It was danced by Nijinsky in the Paris season at the same theatre in 1912, on 20, 22, 24 and 25 May, and in 1913, Nijinsky danced it at the new Théâtre des Champs-Elysées. This was the last season he appeared in Paris. Valentine Gross may have sketched him during any of these seasons. Although more finished than most of her notes 'in action', she would have had a better chance to make at least a good start on this sketch as Nijinsky would be motionless in this pose for several seconds.

Petrushka

Scene II. Petrushka's cell.

Petrushka alone. Nijinsky.

To the music of the piece for piano and orchestra, which was the original *Konzertstück* out of which Stravinsky's and Benois's ballet sprang, the despairing Puppet laments his ugliness, his confinement, and his unrequited love, and protests hysterically against his miserable fate.

Petrushka
Scene II. Petrushka's cell.
Petrushka alone. Nijinsky.
Petrushka in despair.

77

Petrushka

Scene II. Petrushka's cell.

Several studies of Petrushka's dance of frustration. Nijinsky.

Here again, as in the drawings of *Schéhérazade*, Nijinsky appears to be dancing on point, which would be more appropriate for this Puppet than for the voluptuous Slave in the harem. A photograph taken on the set and published in the official programme of the Russian Ballet, confirms this. So does Mme Sokolova, who writes: "Nijinsky's boots had hardened toe-caps and in this scene he did rise on to his toes. Leon [Woizikovsky] did this more than Nijinsky."

Petrushka

Scene II. Petrushka's cell.

The Ballerina and Petrushka. Karsavina and Nijinsky.
The Ballerina comes to pay Petrushka a visit in his cell.
Petrushka's frantic joy scares her away.

One would like to think this was drawn during a
performance, so vivid is the impression it makes. I thought
it might have been done from a famous on-stage photograph of Karsavina and Nijinsky by Bert, but there are
subtle differences – a proof of first-hand observation.

Petrushka

Scene IV. The fair at night.

The Nurse-maids, or Wet-nurses.

One of the set dances which emerges quite naturally like an improvised jollification from the bustle of the crowd, is the dance of the Nurse-maids, with its dipping rhythm.

Aristocratic Russian mothers in the time of Pushkin did not nurse their own babies; they employed peasant women to do it for them. These wore a uniform with a *kokoshnik*, a traditional Russian crown-like head-dress; an apron over spreading skirts and much gold and silver embroidery. The ornate short-skirted coat was discarded for the dance. Characteristics of the buxom and rather pagan dance were the arms folded across the breast and the waving of a handkerchief above the head.

Petrushka

Scene IV. The fair at night.

A Nurse-maid.

She is rotating and waving her handkerchief with a circular motion. Like the previous drawing, this was clearly a note made during the ballet.

The artist worked up her sketches of Nurse-maids, as well as those of the Coachmen that follow, into decorative pen and ink drawings, and made wood-cuts from them.

Petrushka

Scene IV. The fair at night.

Coachmen.

There were two Coachmen who executed a brisk dance, kicking out their legs from a crouching position – the cobblers' step – and flinging out their arms. The artist has scribbled (twice) in the dark, 'pale violet'. This applied to the shirt. The top-hats, jackets, baggy trousers and boots were black.

Petrushka

Scene IV. The fair at night.

A Coachman. George Rosaï.

If this was drawn at the Châtelet Theatre in June 1911, it is George Rosaï, Nijinsky's contemporary from the 1898 class of the Imperial Theatre School, a sturdy little character dancer, at that time aged twenty-one. He had created a sensation in the first season of Russian ballet and opera of 1909 leading the Dance of Buffoons in *Le Pavillon d'Armide*. He died of pneumonia in the winter of 1911–12. The other Coachman, Orlik, wore a beard. Valentine Gross has written what I think is 'bleu et lilas' on the right and something indecipherable on the left.'

Petrushka
Scene IV. The fair at night.
Coachmen.
They are doing the cobblers' step.

Petrushka

Scene IV. The fair at night.

Petrushka about to die. Nijinsky.

Infuriated by Petrushka's admiration for the Ballerina, the Moor (Orlov) has chased him out of the booth and, to the amazement of the merrymaking crowd, struck him down with his scimitar, while the Ballerina holds her head in terror.

Hand outstretched in appeal and accusation, Nijinsky curses God. 'You made me! You gave me a soul! What now?' Then he collapses; and as Cyril Beaumont wrote: 'He went inert like a broken doll. It was only with the greatest difficulty that he was able to raise himself from the ground. His head lolled to and fro as though attached to his neck by a piece of string. His arms jerked feebly. The green glare of a Bengal light turned his features a ghastly green. Then he fell back and rolled over on to his side.'

Whether this was drawn in the theatre or whether the result of 'emotion recollected in tranquillity', it is an extraordinarily vivid impression of a theatrical artist of genius at the climax of one of his great roles. Who, for instance, was on the spot to sketch a scene so vividly described in words by Gordon Craig – Henry Irving pulling off his boots in *The Bells*?

L'Après-midi d'un faune

L'Après-midi d'un faune

Music: Debussy. Choreography: Nijinsky. Décor: Bakst.

The Faun piping. Nijinsky.

Nijinsky as the Faun, at the very beginning of the 'tableau chorégraphique' (his first ballet), reclining on a green bank in the mottled and shimmering forest designed by Bakst, raises the rustic pipe to his lips.

In this drawing and the following ones the artist has instinctively grasped and tried to convey the angular style of movement in profile which Nijinsky had devised to suggest a frieze coming to life. It was this idea which enabled him to make a breakaway from all ballet that had gone before, including Fokine, and take the first step towards abstract composition in dance.

L'Après-midi d'un faune

The Faun reclining. Nijinsky.

Three studies of the Faun on his bank. Top right: with
the pipe. Below: about to pick up his bunch of grapes.
Top left: a slighter sketch of a movement towards the
end of the ballet when the Faun has laid the Nymph's
scarf on the bank and is about to lie on it.

L'Après-midi d'un faune
Another study of the Faun on his bank. Nijinsky.

L'Après-midi d'un faune
The Faun walking. Nijinsky.

Seven Nymphs have come on below, and the seventh has

aroused the desire of the Faun. As the other six bathe her with stylised movements in an imaginary stream to the right, the Faun rises, comes down the slope of his bank to the left of the shallow stage, turns about suddenly, and crosses the stage to the right with a curious automatic walk, his torso almost full-on to the audience, his head, hands and legs in profile.

L'Après-midi d'un faune

The Faun and the Seventh Nymph. Nijinsky and Lydia Nelidova.

The Nymph has discarded three veils before bathing and is wearing a short golden shift (representing nudity), so that when the Faun confronts her she covers her body with angular gestures of modesty.

L'Après-midi d'un faune

The Seventh Nymph kneeling and the Faun jumping.
Nelidova and Nijinsky.

Behind the kneeling Seventh Nymph, the Faun performs
the one jump in the ballet. Notice how the artist has
conveyed the animal quality of the jump Nijinsky
devised: he is a human being with attributes of the goat
and the deer. Nijinsky worked out his ballet with Mme
Bronislava Nijinska, the choreographer's sister, in 1910
and early in 1911, a year before he began to rehearse it
with the company. She herself played the Sixth Nymph,
and told me that she thought this one jump was meant
to be over a brook – the brook in which the Nymph had
bathed, of course. I pointed out that there was indeed a
waterfall painted on the backcloth by Bakst just behind
this line of longitude on the stage.

L'Après-midi d'un faune
Three Nymphs.

L'Après-midi d'un faune

The Sixth Nymph and the Faun. Bronislava Nijinska and Nijinsky.

The Seventh Nymph, desired by the Faun, has fled. Two of her veils have been carried off by the attendant Nymphs; a third remains. This, in the absence of its owner, is to satisfy the Faun's lust. The Sixth Nymph walks on, either to retrieve the third veil or to mock the Faun. He is holding the veil and his look scares her away. Her upraised arms symbolise fear – or at least consternation.

L'Après-midi d'un faune

The Sixth Nymph. Nijinska.

A development of the left-hand figure in the previous sketch.

When Nijinsky's sister became pregnant in 1913 and was obliged to give up her roles, the Sixth Nymph was danced by Diaghilev's first English dancer, Hilda Bewicke.

L'Après-midi d'un faune

The Faun walking, with the veil. Nijinsky.

Alone again, the Faun runs, bearing the veil, left across the stage towards the slope leading to his bank.

101

Right

L'Après-midi d'un faune

The Faun and the veil. Nijinsky.

This is the very end of the ballet. The two drawings are
in the wrong order. Right: the Faun crouches to place
the veil on the ground. Left: he begins to lie down on
top of it.

Left

L'Après-midi d'un faune
The Faun kneeling with the veil. Nijinsky.
Back on his ledge, the Faun kneels and sniffs the veil.
Two drawings.

Curtain-call after L'Après-midi d'un faune
Nijinsky bowing.

Because of the revolutionary nature of the choreography and its abolition of conventional 'grace'; because of the novel, freer relationship of dance to music; and because of Nijinsky's final gesture of stylised orgasm, the ballet created an uproar on the first night. The house was divided between cat-calls and applause. The Russian Ballet had never had such a reception before. A group of stalwart supporters could be heard shouting "Bis!" and this gave Diaghilev the excuse to order the short ballet to be repeated. After all, he wanted to encourage Nijinsky, apart from anything else.

How Calmette denounced the vile thing on the front page of *Le Figaro*, how Rodin and Odilon Redon leapt to its defence, how the police came, how the work was acclaimed in Berlin, London and New York – is a long story.

One doubts if Valentine Gross drew this sketch of the curtain-call after the first night: the excitement would have been too great – and one suspects that she and her friends formed the group of stalwarts whose cries of "Bis!" prompted the encore. Nijinsky danced the Faun altogether fifteen times in Paris (and eight in London).

Daphnis et Chloë

Daphnis et Chloë

Music: Ravel. Choreography: Fokine. Décor: Bakst.

Scene I. The Grove.

Daphnis. Nijinsky.

The first performance of Fokine's *Daphnis* followed a few days after that of Nijinsky's Greek ballet *L'Après-midi d'un faune* at the end of the Paris season of 1912. Diaghilev had commissioned the score from Ravel as early as 1909, but there had been continual postponements, and when Diaghilev allowed Nijinsky to experiment in choreography, Fokine was so indignant that he decided to leave the company. There were to have been four performances of *Daphnis* in Paris, but shortage of rehearsal time and perhaps the scandal arising from Nijinsky's *L'Après-midi* decided Diaghilev to postpone its première, so that there were only two. These were on 8 and 10 June 1912, the last two nights of the season, after which Fokine left the company. The ballet was not given again that year or in 1913. By 1914, the married Nijinsky had been dismissed, and when Diaghilev persuaded Fokine to come back, the latter revived *Daphnis*, and danced it himself, alternately with Karsavina and his wife Vera Fokina, in Monte Carlo, Paris and London.

So this and the following drawings, which could only have been made on 8 or 10 June 1912, on the only two occasions Nijinsky danced *Daphnis*, are of extreme interest and rarity.

First the artist makes an exact note of Nijinsky's simple costume, a white silk belted tunic with a knee-length skirt, the top part crossing over the left shoulder. Then she draws him with his shepherd's crook, and sketches his muscular right leg for good measure.

Daphnis et Chloë
Scene I. The Grove.
Daphnis. Nijinsky.

Valentine Gross did not have to draw in the shepherd's crook for us to realise that Nijinsky was leaning on it, with crossed legs.

Daphnis et Chloë

Scene I. The Grove.

Darkon's dance. Adolf Bolm.

The uncouth herdsman Darkon and the graceful shepherd Daphnis compete in dancing for Chloë's love.

I thought this might be Darkon's dance, but could not prove it, and wondered what the toasting-fork could be that he was holding in his right hand (in contrast to Daphnis's crook). Then a new book by Boris Kochno arrived in which there was an unfamiliar photograph of Bolm in exactly this position. To render his dance bucolic and laughable, Fokine made him show the flat of his hands; and Valentine Gross, drawing in the dark, used the 'toasting-fork' as a shorthand symbol of splayed fingers to remind herself of the nature of his dance. In the drawing on the right, Darkon seems to be standing awkwardly, hands behind his back, to acknowledge applause – which turns out to be derisive.

Daphnis et Chloë

Scene I. The Grove.

Chloë. Karsavina.

Chloë sits on the ground to watch Daphnis dancing. The upper drawing is obscure. Lydia Sokolova wrote: "I loved the calm of Karsavina's Chloë in the first act, and the relaxed way she lay on the ground watching Daphnis dance for her."

Daphnis et Chloë
Scene I. The Grove.
Daphnis. Nijinsky.

Although, again, the crook is not indicated, it is implied
by the uncurled lines representing arms and hands. If
I am right, this is the only surviving evidence that
Nijinsky, at the start of his solo, held the crook down
at arms-length before raising it on to his shoulders and
twining his arms around it – for that is how he held it
during much of the dance. He appears to be standing
with his back to the audience.

Daphnis et Chloë
Scene I. The Grove.
Daphnis. Nijinsky.

Nijinsky poised on the toes of the right foot, with the
left knee raised. Mme Sokolova writes: "Nijinsky's solo
consisted of many jumps – *grand jeté* in various positions,
with the crook moved for each."

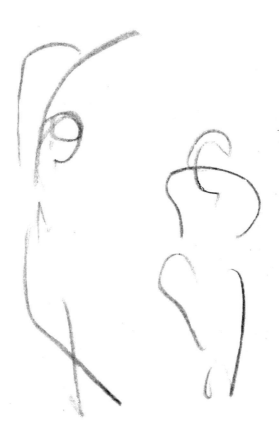

Daphnis et Chloë

Scene I. The Grove.

Daphnis. Nijinsky.

In the left-hand drawing Nijinsky appears to be holding
the (omitted) crook above his head as he executes a step
which consists of dragging one foot behind the other.
The right-hand drawing is harder to interpret.

Daphnis et Chloë

Scene I. The Grove.

Daphnis. Nijinsky.

In the left-hand drawing Nijinsky is jumping, holding the crook above his head. In the right-hand drawing Nijinsky is leaning on the crook.

Daphnis et
Chloé
11

Right

Daphnis et Chloë

Scene I. The Grove.

Daphnis. Nijinsky.

The left-hand drawing shows the basic position of Nijinsky's solo. The shepherd's crook rests on his shoulder and his arms are twined round it. As the left leg, crossed over, carries the body to the right, the head looks back over the left shoulder. Thus we see that even in a 'Greek' ballet, with its freer style of movement, Fokine introduced *épaulement*, the ultimate refinement, which turns ballet from geometry into art. Mme Sokolova writes: "It could be the preparation for a turn."

The right-hand drawing may be of Nijinsky standing, crook in hand, or it may be a spectator of his dance.

Left

Daphnis et Chloë
Scene I. The Grove.
Daphnis.. Nijinsky.

The dancer crosses the stage from right to left, his crook resting on his shoulders. The vertical line to the right is probably a mistake.

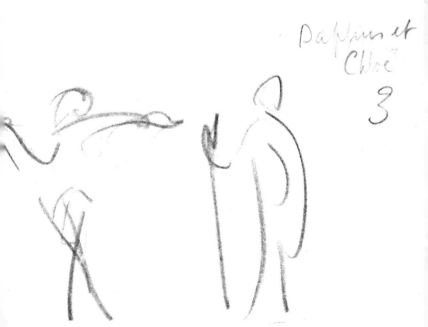

Daphnis et Chloë

Scene I. The Grove.

Daphnis. Nijinsky.

Here, after the curtain has fallen, the artist carries her shorthand notes a step further and tries to produce a more explanatory drawing while Nijinsky's solo with the crook is still fresh in her mind. The two drawings of Nijinsky's back view, side by side, do in fact give a remarkable feeling of movement and of the nature of his dance.

Daphnis et Chloë
Scene I. The Grove.
Chloë. Karsavina.
Two sketches of Karsavina's solo.

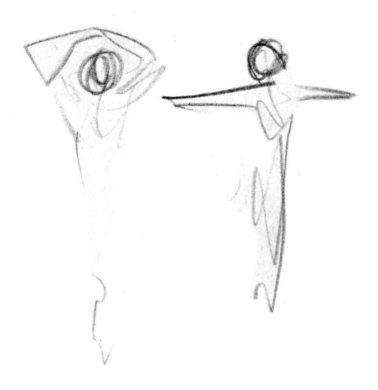

Left

Daphnis et Chloë

Scene I. The Grove.

Daphnis. Nijinsky

Third stage. In the previous drawing Valentine Gross had elaborated her shorthand jotting to give a more descriptive impression of Nijinsky's solo. Here she begins to simplify again in preparation for making a pastel. Two pastels exist – at least I have photographs of them – and they are much more sentimental and less vivid than the drawings. The flimsy white garment now passes over the right shoulder, which is wrong. Against Nijinsky's fillet or *bandeau* the artist has written '*bleu*'.

Daphnis et Chloë

Scene I. The Grove.

Daphnis alone, and Daphnis with Chloë. Nijinsky and Karsavina.

To the left a slightly evolved drawing of Nijinsky's solo (after the event) and to the right an impression of Nijinsky and Karsavina embracing after he has won the dance competition.

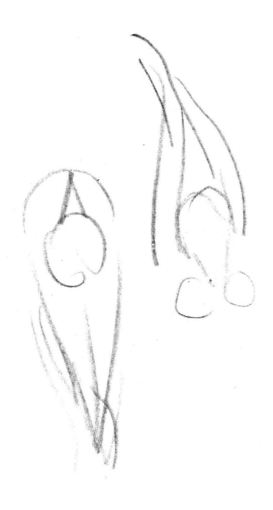

Daphnis et Chloë
Scene I. The Grove.
Probably Lycenion. Ludmila Schollar.

If I am right (and Mme Sokolova thinks the same) this
is the solo of Lycenion, the 'vamp' from the local town,
who tries to lure Daphnis away from Chloë.

Daphnis et Chloë

Scene I. The Grove.

Daphnis and a Nymph. Nijinsky and one of the Nymphs.

As in other sketches, Nijinsky stands leaning on his crook (which is not drawn). The Nymph's yearning pose is exactly like Isadora. In fact there is a drawing by José Clara of Isadora making the same movement.

It is amusing to consider that Fokine, who admired Isadora, and whose choreographic imagination had been liberated by her, was so anxious to prove that she had not influenced him that when Cyril Beaumont was writing the first book about his work, he told Beaumont that she came to Russia in 1907, by which time he had already made two Greek ballets in the free style of movement, *Acis and Galatea* and *Eunice*. Isadora describes in *My Life* her dramatic arrival in Petersburg at dawn, and her meeting of the procession of coffins of the workers shot down by troops on 'Bloody Sunday', January, 1905. Actually, she arrived and gave her first recital in the Salle de la Noblesse in December, 1904. Of course, Isadora's influence on Fokine must have been profound – just as, if she had not danced to Chopin, Gluck and Beethoven, Diaghilev would probably never have commissioned ballets from Ravel, Debussy and Stravinsky. Here, in a drawing not exhibited or published before, of a ballet whose choreography has long been forgotten, we see the most typical Isadora pose 'invented' by Fokine over seven years after the great American pioneer had changed his life.

Daphnis et Chloë
Scene I. The Grove.
A Nymph.
One of the three Nymphs who appear to Daphnis when
he is lamenting the kidnapping of Chloë by pirates.

Daphnis et Chloë
Scene I. The Grove.
Daphnis. Nijinsky.

This seems to be Daphnis, after the capture of Chloë, crawling away and wanting to die.

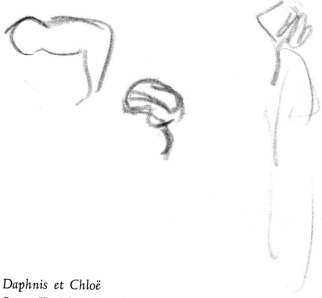

Daphnis et Chloë
Scene II. The pirates' camp.
Chloë. Karsavina.

Chloë in despair after her capture. Unfinished sketches of her coiffure on the left.

Daphnis et Chloë
Scene II. The pirates' camp.
Chloë. Karsavina.

Forced to dance by the pirates, she expresses her desperation. Here we can see not only just what the dancer's Greek dress was like, the material caught in three places, but also the passionate curves into which she flung her body and arms.

Le Sacre du printemps

Le Sacre du printemps

Music: Stravinsky. Choreography: Nijinsky. Décor: Roerich.

Scene I.

The first performance of *Le Sacre* at the newly built Théâtre des Champs-Elysées took place on 29 May, 1913, and caused what was probably the fiercest battle in the history of the theatre. The novelty of the music and choreography was too much for the elegant occupants of the boxes, who expressed their disgust vociferously, to be shouted down by the bohemian *avant-garde*. Not only insults but blows were exchanged, and the houselights were turned on; but although for most of the time the music was inaudible, the ballet was danced through to the end. The scornful critics called it 'Le Massacre du printemps'. Valentine Gross was standing in the dress circle and there could have been no possibility of her drawing that evening. At the three subsequent performances in Paris, however, she filled several notebooks with jottings in blue crayon, of which this is one: a group, with a single dancer on the left. This is included to show how the artist recorded successive phases of the choreography while the ballet was in progress.

Left

Le Sacre du printemps

Scene I.

Two costumes.

The costumes for both men and women were long smocks, caught up at the waist. All the dancers wore leggings. The girls had plaits and some of the men wore pointed caps. Most of the girls wore red, stencilled with varied bands of primitive pattern in many colours; the men wore white, similarly decorated.

On the left is a girl's costume, inscribed '*Fleurs jaunes au corsage*' – yellow flowers on the body. On the right a man's costume, the hat being described as '*marron*', that is, dark reddish-brown, and the border of the skirt '*mauve*'.

Right
Le Sacre du printemps
Scene II. Danse Sacrale.
Pilz.
A rapid sketch made in the theatre of two of the Chosen Virgin's movements in her final solo.

Le Sacre du printemps

Scene II. Mystic Circles of Young Girls.

Five studies of female dancers including Maria Pilz.

In the second scene, one girl is chosen from a group to be sacrificed to propitiate the Harvest God. She dances herself to death. Mme Sokolova, who, with Dame Marie Rambert, was one of the girls in the group [in Massine's 1920 version of *Le Sacre* she was the Chosen Virgin] writes: "These are the positions we took at the opening of the second scene – all facing out, moving anti-clockwise, about twelve of us." As they moved round, the girls changed from the pose drawn here, top centre, to that on the top left and back again. "All feet were turned inwards for these shuffling steps; we rose on half point as the new position was taken – a gradual slow movement."

The two drawings at the foot are of the pose assumed by the Chosen Virgin (Pilz) as she waited to begin her frantic Danse Sacrale.

Over page

Le Sacre du printemps

Scene II. Danse Sacrale and other numbers.

Pilz and others.

The drawing top left (a tidier version of that on page 134), and probably all the other single figures, are of Pilz in her final solo, but the other girls assumed similar poses at the beginning of the scene in the dance called 'Mystic Circles'. In the centre, a group of men, possibly from the first scene.

Le Sacre du printemps
Scene II. Danse Sacrale.
Pilz.

The drawing top right is a developed version of ones produced on the two preceding pages. Probably all studies are of Pilz in her final dance, but Mme Sokolova points out that all the girls made similar movements at the beginning of the scene during the ritual of choosing, called 'Mystic Circles of Young Girls'.